Journey
to the
Millennium
and bey

Reflections, prayers
of Christian w(

Collated by the Ecumenical Committee of
the National Board of Catholic Women
Line drawings by Anne McGough

MCCRIMMONS
Great Wakering Essex England

First published in Great Britain in 1998 by
McCrimmon Publishing Co. Ltd.
10-12 High Street, Great Wakering, Essex SS3 0EQ

Telephone 01702–218956
Fax 01702–216082
Email: mccrimmons@dial.pipex.com

ISBN 0 85597 596 2

Cover design by Nick Snode
Typeset in ITC Garramond Light 11/13pt
Reprographics by Anagram Litho Ltd, Southend-on-Sea, Essex
Printed on 90gsm Fineblade Cartridge
Printed by Anthony Rowe Limited., Reading, Berkshire

ACKNOWLEDGEMENTS

We would like to thank all those who have granted permission for use of material in this book. Every effort has been made to trace and identify copyright holders and to secure necessary permission for reprinting. If we have erred in any respect, we apologise and would be glad to make any necessary amendments in subsequent editions of this book.

Rev Mair Bowen –	*God the Source of Hope*, (WWDP)
	Loving God (and Welsh translation), (ibid)
	Welsh translation of *Roll back the Stone*, (ibid)
F. Mary Callan –	*Woman at the Well* from PATCHWORK OF LOVE
	Scraps: the Presence of God from GOSPEL PATCHWORK
Janice Clark –	*Where are you in the time of our troubles* from OCEANS OF PRAYER by
	Maureen Edwards and Jan S. Pickard, by permission
	of National Christian Education Council
Gillian Crow –	*Enduring to the End* from GRAINS OF SALT AND RAYS OF LIGHT –
	REFLECTIONS ON ST MATTHEW'S GOSPEL by Gillian Crow, (St Paul's)
Pat Durrant –	*Fourth Station of the Cross, Jesus meets his Blessed Mother,* (UCM, 1993)
Shelagh Grey –	*A Mother's Silence* from VOL.12 ASSOCIATION OF CATHOLIC WOMEN REVIEW
	(Sept.1992) under the name Ann O'Neil
Linda Jones –	*The Excluded* from Celebrating One World, (CAFOD)
	Chains of Debt from Debt Vigil, (ibid)
	Healing Touch, (ibid)
Julian of Norwich –	an extract from the LONGER REVELATIONS which form a postscript to the
	shorter version of SIXTEEN REVELATIONS OF DIVINE LOVE as
	translated and edited by Anna Maria Reynolds CP in A SHEWING OF
	GOD'S LOVE (Longmans Green)
Rachel Lampard &	*Lord, we pray for those living on the edge of communities,* and
Jennie Richmond –	*For Forgiveness* produced for HOMELESSNESS SUNDAY 1998
	on behalf of CHAS and CNHC (copy packs available from CHAS)
Janet Morley –	*Roll Back the Stone* from BREAD OF TOMORROW
	(SPCK & Christian Aid 1992)
Sue Norris –	*Send forth your Spirit* from RENEWAL IN THE SPIRIT – A PEOPLE OF HOPE
	(Portsmouth Diocese)
	There is an enormous variety of gifts from RENEWAL IN SPIRIT, (ibid)
Petal Mary O'Hea –	*The Journey* from …OF MIND AND MATTER, (Envoi Poets Publication)
Edith Reyntiens &	
Jean Mayland –	*Holy Mother Hilda* from Worship BOOK OF FORWARD TO THE PROMISED
	COMMUNITY CONFERENCE, DURHAM 1998, (CCBI)
Annabel	
Shilson-Thomas –	*Compassionate God* from CELEBRATING ONE WORLD, (CAFOD)
Janet Stuart –	*Prayer* from POEMS by Janet Erskine Stuart.
	Edited by Maud Monaghan (Sands & Co) 1951
Dorothy Webster –	*Hope* – extract reprinted from THE FRIEND
	19 March 1971 with kind permission

The Scripture quotations contained herein are from *The New Revised Standard Version of the Bible*, Anglicised Edition, © 1989, 1995 by the DIVISION OF CHRISTIAN EDUCATION OF THE NATIONAL COUNCIL OF CHURCHES OF CHRIST IN THE UNITED STATES OF AMERICA, and are used by permission. All rights reserved.

INTRODUCTION

In his letter 'Tertio Millennio Adveniente', Pope John Paul II invites us to prepare for the Jubilee Year 2000. When the National Board of Catholic Women was considering how it might best prepare for the Jubilee, one of our members put forward the idea that Christian women of England and Wales could be given the opportunity to write their own prayers and reflections for the nine months leading up to the Millennium and have them published in a book. The suggestion of nine months was made because this is the normal pregnancy time, the time of preparation, anticipation, waiting and fulfilment. It was felt that Catholic women particularly were rarely invited or had the opportunity to express their spiritual thoughts in writing. However an early decision was made that our sisters from other Christian churches would be invited to contribute, hence the Ecumenical Committee of the Board took up the challenge to plan the book and to collate the contributions.

A structure was agreed and circulated to our organisations, dioceses and associated groups. The response we received was tremendous and we are most grateful to all who contributed and shared their thoughts and experiences so generously. Unfortunately we were unable to include all the contributions because there were too many for the size of the book. The Ecumenical Committee had the difficult task of selecting submissions. It was a long and arduous but very rewarding experience, and we were surprised by some aspects of the response. We received a large number of poems on the theme of the Annunciation, showing that this event is of real significance to many women. We were also surprised and delighted that most of the material we received was original.

We hope that you will read and use the book in the time leading up to the great Jubilee and beyond. The contents speak for themselves. We aimed to make the book available to all women, in a useful size, neither too big nor too glossy.

There are many people that the Board must thank. First our thanks go to two members of the original Millennium Committee, Mary McHugh and Celia Capstick,who steered it through the initial stages; then the Ecumenical Committee of the Board which has done most of the work – Mavis Bailey, Joan Cheetham, Sister Fidelis Daly, Jackie Foster, Sister Fanny Martin, Janet Ward and particularly Mary Brogan, the committee convener who has inspired us all with her dedication and enthusiasm for the project. We must also thank our artist, Anne McGough, for her helpfulness, suggestions and patience. We wish to acknowledge the support of the Women's World Day of Prayer Committee and Pauline Butcher, convener of the Women's Inter-Church Council, who so willingly circulated the prayer book information to its members. Finally we should thank the Society of Jesus for its interest and support, and the Order of Cross and Passion for its most generous financial contributions which have encouraged us and have helped to make the publication possible.

Freda Lambert, President NBCW

The Ecumenical Committee would like to record its thanks to Freda Lambert not only as a member of the Committee but for her unfailing support and encouragement in this project.

CONTENTS

CONTENTS

SECTION I

Annunciation, Passion and Death, Resurrection

SECTION II

Pentecost and the work of the Holy Spirit in Ordinary Time

CONTENTS

SECTION III

Advent, Incarnation, Reconciliation, and the coming of the Kingdom

CONTENTS

SECTION I

Annunciation, Passion and Death, Resurrection

God so loved the world that He gave His only Son

God so loved the created universe, the sea,
the sky, the land, the people –
The sea with its beauty, its power, its myriad
varieties of life,
The sky in its majesty, its splendour, its vastness
and its mystery,
The land of mountains, valleys, rivers, the cities,
towns and villages and all that they contain
of life and of living,
Men and women in their greatness and their weakness.

So good did God find the work of creation and so needy
did the human family seem in their living in God's world
that God chose to assume human form.
And so by the message of an angel
God became a foetus in the womb of a woman.

God experienced the wonder of growing into a human shape.
God felt the weakness of a baby
and the dependence that weakness causes.
God knew the tenderness, the joy, the care of loving parents.
God grew as a child and waxed strong, full of wisdom,
And the grace of God was in him.
He went down to Nazareth and was subject to them.
For thirty years God lived, worked, ate, drank, slept and prayed.

We have no record of what happened during these precious years.
We can but wonder at a mystery.

Fidelis Daly C.P.

Luke 1: 26–38

In the sixth month the angel Gabriel was sent by God to a town in Galilee called Nazareth, to a virgin engaged to a man whose name was Joseph, of the house of David. The virgin's name was Mary. And he came to her and said, "Greetings, favoured one! The Lord is with you." But she was much perplexed by his words and pondered what sort of greeting this might be. The angel said to her, "Do not be afraid, Mary, for you have found favour with God. And now, you will conceive in your womb and bear a son, and you will name him Jesus. He will be great, and will be called the Son of the Most High, and the Lord God will give to him the throne of his ancestor David. He will reign over the house of Jacob for ever, and of his kingdom there will be no end." Mary said to the angel, "How shall this be, since I am a virgin?" The angel said to her, "The Holy Spirit will come upon you, and the power of the Most High will overshadow you; therefore the child to be born will be holy; he will be called Son of God. And now, your relative Elizabeth in her old age has also conceived a son; and this is the sixth month for her who was said to be barren. For nothing will be impossible with God." Then Mary said, "Here I am, the servant of the Lord; let it be with me according to your word." Then the angel departed from her.

John 1: 14

And the Word became flesh and lived among us, and we have seen his glory, the glory as of a father's only son, full of grace and truth.

A *Millennium Magnificat*

I feel it all around me
and within me;
The Presence of God.
His hand, He laid upon me.
His angel, He sent to me,
and in one all revealing moment
It was made known to me;
Who I am,
My purpose,
The reason for my being.
I was made whole
Then.
And happiness flows
and courses through me.
And through me, through Him;
Through Jesus, through my baby –
Jesus.
I am, each moment, alive
For Him.
A temple to house Him.
My breath gives Him breath,
The food I eat, nourishes Him.
This miracle is made possible
Because God is Almighty
and looks not on what we deserve.
All I had to do was say 'Yes'.

Patricia Chamberlain

Gratia Plena

My soul now magnifies the Lord,
The Lord, the Father and giver of life
Life that breathes and stirs in the secret place
True flesh of God knit together
Here in my womb.

Magnificat, magnificat
Spring sunshine warming and bathing the earth
In light, as the strong sun of righteousness
Rises in me, Christ, Son of God,
My Saviour.

Sweet bird of peace sings in my ears
At dawn of new day, herald of God's grace
Flowing in a dry and barren desert
Restoring, refreshing my soul,
Gratia plena.

Over-shadowing power of the most High
Swelling of ripening grain, gold and glorious
Fearful, wonderful Spirit, uphold me
Through waves of terror and nausea,
Bringing your peace.

Angel's strange message ringing in my ears
How can I not embrace your word my Lord?
Gift of life growing daily within me
As fresh buds and blossoms flourish
All round me.

Pray for us now, Holy Mother of God
That we too may humbly accept the gift
Of His gracious, blest word and will for us
In the midst of our life and death
Amen, Amen.

Barbara Winstanley

Luke 1: 46–55

And Mary said:
"My soul magnifies the Lord,
and my spirit rejoices in God my Saviour,
for he has looked with favour
on the lowliness of his servant.
Surely, from now on all generations will call me blessed;
for the Mighty One has done great things for me,
and holy is his name.
His mercy is for those who fear him
from generation to generation.
He has shown strength with his arm;
he has scattered the proud in the thoughts of their hearts.
He has brought down the powerful from their thrones
and lifted up the lowly;
He has filled the hungry with good things
and sent the rich away empty.
He has helped his servant Israel,
in remembrance of his mercy,
according to the promises he made to our ancestors,
to Abraham and to his descendants for ever."

The Annunciation

1   The child in her womb kicked
    And the Mother-God knew that the time had come for
    Her child to break into the world
    That he too had helped to create.
    No 'God from God' nor 'Light from Light' this,
    But 'Womb from Womb', 'Mother to Mother'.
    And she wept for the child whom she
    would not suckle, nor comfort,
    but give to another while still warm in her womb.
    She gave him only her spirit of wisdom and passion
    And another mother whose gentleness could never be measured.

    See how she loves us, oh fulness of creation:
    We take of Her body:
    It has been given up for us.

2   And so God's spirit hovered over the earth,
    Like once it had hovered over the chaos.
    And in the noise, it found a place of stillness and peace,
    which was Mary's soul.

    And Mary was betrothed to Joseph,
    But she did not think of him,
    Only of God and her desire for God.

    And the Spirit asked her
    If she would bear God's child.
    And in her the spirit found a space
    Which waited to be filled with
    The utter fulness of God.

And Mary felt passion and resistance
at the same time,
But when she sensed a new life
beginning to move in her,
She felt at peace.

And the Spirit remained with her
and the child of God.

3   And so God's love for us ceased to be mere words,
But became the one, true Word;
The boy-God, who existed before time ever was,
and will be still when time is no more,

   – was made visible   – so we might see him with our eyes,
   – was made tangible – so we might touch him with our hands,
   – was made audible   – so we might hear him in our hearts.

One with us
One of us
One with the womb who bore him,
and One with the womb of God.

He was at once
human frailty
and power divine,
And,
bursting into our lives
one night,
like sparks of crackling coal,
Jesus, the Word, was uttered;
and with his breath
he set
our
darkened
sky
aflame.   *Suzy Brouard*

1 John 1: 1–2

We declare to you what was from the beginning, what we have heard, what we have seen with our eyes, what we have looked at and touched with our hands, concerning the word of life – this life was revealed, and we have seen it and testify to it, and declare to you the eternal life that was with the Father and was revealed to us.

Mary was immaculate,
without sin.
She was – is – blessed among women,
Holy Mary,
Queen of Heaven,
Mother of God,
Star of the Sea,
Mystical Rose…
But I think she was also like you and me,
like all of us, expecting our first child,
confused by conflicting emotions:
fear and hope,
wonder and anxiety,
discomfort and excitement…
And overriding all of these
she must have felt
astonishing tenderness
for something, someone
not yet seen, not yet held,
not yet born to change our world.
Hail Mary, sister and friend.

Anthea Dove

Elizabeth's Song

The setting sun of ages past
dipped at her dawning light
and as she called, my spirit soared
and sensed her infant's might
the child within me also knew
and leapt for sheer delight.

I greeted Mary, young and fair
for all our ancient race
and she gave glory back to God
in praises full of grace.
She shone in joy and blazing faith
at God's most bounteous might
and as we gazed on wondrous times
the world seemed full of light.

She sang in gladness of new hope
of 'God with us' in awe
and then I knew what all my years
of waiting had been for
how Kings had prayed and prophets sighed
to see what I now saw.

My own dear one so blessed would be
a voice to point the way,
and smooth the paths of wilderness
until Emmanuel's day.
I welcomed Mary young and fair
for all the human race
and she replied by praising God
the fountain of all grace.

Rosemary Keith

Mary pondering
'what could all this mean?'
storing all these things
letting them simmer
not trying to work out
but to absorb and become a part.

Mary treasured all these things
Of great value to ponder lovingly
on a treasure.
May I treasure like Mary.

Martine Patoir

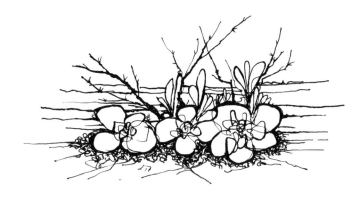

Continuum

Travelling with your child in the dark
did you see the signpost
know the road?

Did you hear your own pain
in your son's birth cry?
Did you hear mine?

Did you learn the knack
of curving his head against your breast
at my breast?

Have you felt the flutterings,
the movements of love
with the pull of his mouth?

Mavis Carter

Isaiah 12: 2

Surely God is my salvation;
    I will trust and will not be afraid,
    for the Lord God is my strength and
        my might
he has become my salvation.

Creation

A snowdrop bursts so prettily through the dampened earth,
Nestling sedately between the grassy shoots.
Sunlit rays softly enfold each fragile flower –
A vision of hope, an end to darkness –
A pointer to safe, warm, productive times,
Creation is beautiful – ALLELUIA !

Bombs drop, the smell of gas, fuel, cordite.
A harsh clashing and a fusion of two lovers
Turning together, and the fear of Death, Pregnancy,
Sickness, isolation, and a lonely contemplation
Of a land splintered by MAN.
A baby struggles not to be born.
Creation is harsh – ALLELUIA !

Let me through ! Don't let me out!
Tension between the worlds of dark safety
and unknown fearsome light.
To be pulled inexorably towards
A growth, a blossoming, a fading and a dying.
To be drawn towards another hidden world.
Creation is moving – ALLELUIA !

Jay Adams

Baby

You came to lodge in room I made,
bestowed you in my breast,
and might you gently suck me to
an everlasting rest;
for how shall I lay to my shoulder
your tassels, your rose to my cheek,
as pearled-so-exquisitely boulder
you raise on a reed so weak,
when limbs as silken, eyeballs, flesh
haven of all desires,
glutted at Treblinka the kilns
and fatted Auschwitz's fires?

Anna Rist

Psalm 102: 1, 3–5, 18–21

Hear my prayer, O Lord;
let my cry come to you.

For my days pass away like smoke,
and my bones burn like a furnace.
My heart is stricken and withered like grass;
I am too wasted to eat my bread.
Because of my loud groaning
my bones cling to my skin.

Let this be recorded for a generation to come,
so that a people yet unborn may praise the Lord:
that he looked down from his holy height,
from heaven the Lord looked at the earth,
to hear the groans of the prisoners,
to set free those who were doomed to die;
so that the name of the Lord may be declared in Zion,
and his praise in Jerusalem.

I am currently expecting twins and am about
to become a mother for the first time. My babies
are held safely within the environment of the
womb and have everything that they need in
order to grow and develop, they can turn upside
down and yet they are safe.
This is how we are held by God and yet we
sometimes fail to trust 'that all shall be well'.
When my babies are born I shall feed them
with my body and we shall enter into the most
significant and important unity together; much
of their healthy development will depend upon
how this task is negotiated. When I put this
together with the actual experience of giving birth...
these words come into mind:

Jesus took a loaf of bread he broke it... and said,
"Take, eat; this is my body"...
Then he took a cup... saying,
"Drink from it, all of you; for this is my blood of the
covenant, which is poured out for many for the
forgiveness of sins" (Matthew 26: 26–28)

I feel that the relationship of the mother and
child mirrors that of Jesus and myself.
Being a woman has so much to teach us about
God and yet I never hear it preached about.

taken from 'Do not be Afraid' NBCW 1992

Transubstantiation in Reverse

Saint John wrote: "In the beginning was the Word, and the Word was with God, and the Word was God"
Mary was the Mother of God, therefore she was the Mother of the Word.

"The Word was God, and without Him was made nothing that was made…"
God is not only within us but within the bread and wine given for all.
As a man, at the last supper before His death, Christ gave Himself to the world in the form of bread and wine.
As a child, when He came to earth, Mary formed His body before birth from bread, wine and fruits of the earth created by God.
She grew Him to manhood with bread she had baked, and wine made from local grapes. These gifts of nature, made by the Word, formed God on Earth within Mary's womb. God was the Word but Mary used God's gifts of creation to build her son's body and added L for Love to the Word to make World.

So the young Mary held her God, the Word and all creation within her for nine months before presenting her sacrifice to mankind.
When Christ offered Himself as bread and wine before His return to Heaven, he was reversing what his own Mother had done for Him to bring Him from Heaven to live as a man on earth.

Mary Daniels

Three Prayers from within Prison

Dear Lord, Your house I visited yesterday
And my heart was full of things to say
But as Your doors opened wide to let me in
All I could think of was my sin.
It was the Carol Service that brought me to visit You
And the PO had requested me to read a verse or two
My heart was heavy and my eyes wet with tears
Why did she choose me, did she realise my fears.
I tried so hard to sing out loud
But I could not make a sound
I'm sure You knew. I felt You close by
I felt without You there, I would surely die.
Are You still with me now I ASK
Watching me through my daily tasks
Will You hold my hand when I walk into the dock
My sins to confess aloud and clear
I need to know that You are near
For years I've cast You aside
Broken Your commandments, stolen and lied.
But as I spoke to You that day
I knew that You, with me, would always stay.

(Written by Margaret on Christmas Day 1985)

[PO = Prison Officer]

Four high walls cold and bare
You look around there's no-one there
A hollow voice that has no face
An echoing noise about the place.
For myself I do not mind
But heartache for my babes left behind
It's my fault, I'm to blame
But they suffer, just the same.
Lonely hours to think of my past
The shame and sorrow I have cast
Could it be but a bad dream
Not as frightening as it may seem?
I pinch myself to no avail
And accept the fact that I'm in jail

(from Risley)

God I pray to you
To keep my family safe
And guide them on the right path
Give them strength to carry on
During these difficult times
Let them learn to forgive
As You do
And to be kind to others
Amen

Carina

Reproaches

My people, what have I done to you? or in what way
have I grieved you? Answer me.

Because I led you out of the land of Egypt, you have
prepared a cross for your Saviour.

Because I led you through the desert for forty years,
and gave you manna to eat, and led you into a land
sufficient for your needs, you have prepared a cross for your Saviour.

What more should I have done for you that I have not
done? Indeed I planted you, my chosen and most
beautiful vineyard, and you have become for me
excessively bitter, for you have quenched my thirst with
vinegar and pierced the side of your Saviour with a lance.

I scourged Egypt with its first-born for your sake, and after
scourging me, you betrayed me.
My people, what have I done to you? Or in what way
have I grieved you? Answer me.

I led you out of Egypt, plunging Pharaoh into the Red
Sea, and you handed me over to the chief priests.
My people, what have I done to you? Or in what way
have I grieved you? Answer me.

In front of you I opened the sea, and you have opened
my side with a lance.
My people, what have I done to you? Or in what way
have I grieved you? Answer me.

I went before you in a pillar of cloud, but you
have led me to the praetorium of Pilate.
My people, what have I done to you? Or in what way
have I grieved you? Answer me.

I have nourished you with manna all through the
desert, but you have subjected me to blows and scourges.
My people, what have I done to you? Or in what way
have I grieved you? Answer me.

I gave you the water of salvation from the rock to drink,
but you gave me gall and vinegar.
My people, what have I done to you? Or in what way
have I grieved you? Answer me.

I struck the Canaan kings for your sake, but you have
struck my head with a reed.
My people, what have I done to you? Or in what way
have I grieved you? Answer me.

I gave you a royal sceptre, but you gave my head a
crown of thorns.
My people, what have I done to you? Or in what way
have I grieved you? Answer me.

I raised you up to great heights, but you have hung me
on the gibbet of the cross.
My people, what have I done to you ? Or in what way
have I grieved you? Answer me.

(translated by Mary Brogan)

Fourth Station of the Cross
– Jesus Meets His Blessed Mother

Stumbling down the road, through the crowds, one face stood out – His Mother. Their eyes met and through her silent tears He felt the compassion she shared with Him. The joy of meeting overshadowed by the impending doom.

My Son, why have they done this to you, you who only came among us to bring hope for our future. You suffered physical pain and humiliation for them and yet they cannot see the degradation they cause is against themselves.

There will be other Mothers like me, treading their own personal Via Dolorosa; standing and watching whilst their sons give their lives to help humanity. Like me the torment of their anguish will be public, denied the dignity of bearing their grief within the privacy of their own home.

Jesus, grant them the comfort and peace of your love and enable them to accept their sorrow as a true sign of faith.

Pat Durrant

From Life to Death

A tormented figure of death,
Looming like a shadow over the gaping crowd of his killers.
The sky mourning with blackness,
As it sweeps silently across the pitiful figure,
Of a man who once lived.

Once praised,
Once worshipped,
Once loved,
He is no more, now a decaying corpse,
Hanging grimly from a wood rotten cross.

They called him a God once.
Can you believe it now?
Can you?
Look at him.
Does he look like a God?

Well! What is your answer?
Yes or
No?
Or are you not sure?
Then look again…
And again.

What do you see?
Do you see a man in a white robe,
With pearls around his neck,
And angels at his feet?
Or do you see something different?

Different indeed is the sight before you.
A sight of a man degraded by his own people,
Mocked at and spat at,
Flogged and crucified,
And left to die.

And yet you did nothing,
Except to face the dying body of this innocent man.
Are you a coward or a fool?
Look again at this man.
Look again…
Must he look like a God to be a God?

Rita Rytka (1960–1979) written at the age of 14

Psalm 22: 14–21

I am poured out like water,
and all my bones are out of joint;
my heart is like wax;
it is melted within my breast;
my mouth is dried up like a potsherd ,
and my tongue sticks to my jaws;
you lay me in the dust of death.

For dogs are all around me;
a company of evildoers encircles me.
My hands and feet have shrivelled;
I can count all my bones.
They stare and gloat over me;
they divide my clothes among themselves,
and for my clothing they cast lots.

But you, O Lord, do not be far away!
O my help, come quickly to my aid!
Deliver my soul from the sword,
my life from the power of the dog!
Save me from the mouth of the lion!

Easter People

Good Friday dawns so bright and clear, as it would have done
    in Our Lord's time,
I wonder what He was thinking as He made that final climb?
We have prayed the Stations around the Church, and shared
    His painful hours,
We weep for the Man who was perfect, as His blood for us outpours.

Would we have been like Simon, who helped with the Cross
    on the way?
Or would we have been like so many are now
    'It does not concern us,' they say.
Would we have wiped His poor face with a cloth?
    just like Veronica did.
Would we have helped Him to get to His feet?
    as under His burden He slid.

Would we have tossed for the robe He was wearing? or grabbed for
    a souvenir,
Or cowardly turned our eyes away, pretending that
    we were not there,
On Saturday night we wait with Him, it is the least that we can do,
Tomorrow we will hear He is risen and pray one day we will share
    that too.

Jean Sherriff

Myrrh – A Reflection

Three Kings came
Cradled the Babe in bejewelled arms,
Gave of their gifts and left by a different path.
I wonder at their gifts as I
Cradle the Babe in my homespun arms.

Gold is a useful gift.
The Babe likes the glitter and clink of it
And we are glad of the security it offers;
As we walk a different path to a new land.
I cradle the Babe in my lap
And wonder at God's mercy on it.

Frankincense – what to make of that then
Sweet smell and curled smoke rising.
A fitting sacrifice for God's Son in Jerusalem's Temple.
"A sword shall pierce my heart!"
I wonder at those two old dears and their words surprising.

Myrrh – myrrh causes my heart to tremble
As I cradle the Babe against my breast.
Myrrh betokens all the world's pain and all the world's loss
Anointing the dead – ah let me hold Him yet awhile –
Sweet, sweet child, grow not away too fast.
Abba, heavenly Father, let me know what is best.

Myrrh anoints all the world's pain and all the world's loss.
"Blessed are they who mourn for they shall be comforted!"
"Talitha cumi – give her something to eat."
"If you want you can cure me" "Of course I want to, be cured."
"Do not cry. – Young man I say to you get up."
As salve takes the sting from the pain
Abba's son and mine restores them to life again?

I wonder at this gift of myrrh
As I watch his body on the gibbet racked.
My heart pierced by the pain he bears,
His head upon my breast and he, inert upon my lap.
Once more I embrace my Son and wonder what we lacked
That Abba allowed it thus.

I wonder at this gift of myrrh
As I walk with the women to the tomb
How his body we need to anoint – the last comfort give.
And as I grasp the myrrh's portent; believe: in entering the pain
Break the barriers to find him living again.
Oh Abba, loving Father Amen, Amen.

Anne Hine, rscj

Luke 23: 50–56

Now there was a good and righteous man named Joseph, who, though a member of the council, had not agreed to their plan and action. He came from the Jewish town of Arimathea, and he was waiting expectantly for the kingdom of God. This man went to Pilate and asked for the body of Jesus. Then he took it down, wrapped it in a linen cloth, and laid it in a rock-hewn tomb where no one had ever been laid. It was the day of Preparation, and the sabbath was beginning. The women who had come with him from Galilee followed, and they saw the tomb and how his body was laid. Then they returned, and prepared spices and ointments.On the sabbath they rested according to the commandment.

Roll Back the Stone

When we are all despairing;
when the world is full of grief;
when we see no way ahead,
and hope has gone away;
Roll back the stone.

Although we fear change;
although we are not ready;
although we'd rather weep
and run away;
Roll back the stone.

Because we're coming
   with the women;
because we hope
   where hope is vain;
because you call us from
   the grave
and show us the way:
Roll back the stone.

Treigla Ymaith Y Maen

Pan gyrhaeddwn ben ein tennyn;
pan fo'r byd yn llawn gofidiau;
pan na welwn y ffordd ymlaen
a'n gobaith wedi pylu;
Treigla ymaith y maen.

Er inni ofni newid;
er mai amharod ydym;
er mai gwell fyddai gennym wylo
a rhedeg i ffwrdd;
Treigla ymaith y maen.

Am inni ddod gyda'r gwragedd;

am inni obeithio lle mae gobaith
   yn gwegian;

am iti'n galw ni o'r bedd
a dangos inni'r ffordd:
Treigla ymaith y maen

Janet Morley (Welsh translation by Mair Bowen)

45

Running to Tell the Good News

We ran,
   how we ran!
      How could we not?
         Knowing what we did,
            Seeing what we had seen.
"Quick, Mary, Joanna, quick,
Pick up your skirts and run,
to tell, the others, the good news."
Now!
   Now!
My heart will explode, surely,
   it is like falling in love,
      only ten times greater,
         and running as well,
I feel as though
I will die –
No!
   No !
He is not dead,
   He is risen.

Wait! Wait! Wait till I see
Their faces
   light up with joy
"Mary, Joanna,   quick,   quick!"

Running, stumbling,
no longer in fear,
but in joy!

Can you imagine?
My heart is beating
LOUD,   LOUD –
Can they hear it?
    Already – can they sense it?
        Already – do they know it?

Here, we are,
we have arrived.
I cannot talk, breathless, joy,   too great,
I manage,   hardly,   to utter the words:
"He is risen" and again, "HE IS RISEN!"

And as I stop
to catch my breath,
I see,
the men –
their faces
    dull and dismayed,
and their eyes
do not
    light up,
but look only
as if to say:
'What are we
    to do
        with these
            hysterical
                women?'

Suzy Brouard

A Mother's Silence

Still, in the silence,
    Yahweh's voice!
Still, in the silence,
    "Mary a choice."
Still, in the silence,
    Annunciation.
Spirit-filled silence,
    "Thy will be done."

Hard is my silence,
    heart filled with joy.
Hard is my silence,
    see it's a boy.
Hard is my silence,
    knowing God's son.
Love-filled silence,
    "Thy will be done."

Wrapped in my silence,
    In God he will grow.
Wrapped in my silence,
    the Father he'll know.
Wrapped in my silence,
    his life's work begun.
Faith-filled silence,
    "Thy will be done."

Painful my silence,
    my son's gone away.
Painful my silence,
    hear what they say?
Painful my silence,
    scoff, scorn, hearts that shun.
Wound-filled silence,
    "Thy will be done."

Screaming in silence,
    – too much to bear.
Screaming in silence,
    his flesh they tear.
Screaming in silence,
    cross-fast he's hung,
Searing silence
    "Thy will be done."

Clasp him in silence,
    flesh of my flesh.
Clasp him in silence,
    silence of death.
Clasp him in silence,
    Son, oh my son!
Grief-filled silence,
    "Thy will be done."

Think of the silence,
    cold in the tomb.
Think of the silence,
    warm in my womb.
Think of the silence,
    promise all gone.
Life-stilled silence,
    "Thy will be done."

Here, from that silence,
    – can it be true?
Hear from that silence,
    "My peace with you."
Back from that silence,
    Resurrection!
Glory-filled silence,
    "Thy will be done."

Shelagh Grey

Easter

Always waiting
for birth
for growth
for change
for anointing,
– the women
always preparing
always ready
– now called
to be bearers
of Good News –
Christ is risen!
Go and tell
the brothers!
Bearers of the
seed of hope.

Martine Patoir

Matthew 28: 9–10

Suddenly Jesus met them and said, 'Greetings!' And they came
to him, took hold of his feet, and worshipped him. Then Jesus
said to them, 'Do not be afraid; go tell my brothers to go to
Galilee; there they will see me.'

Hope

We need hope for the future
in our nostalgia
for half forgotten summer days
long past.

We need hope of pardon
in our regrets
which drift through our minds
like autumn clouds of dying leaves.

We need hope of comfort
in our fears and anxieties
fed by the long hours of darkness
in winter.

Hope of the World,
born in dark midwinter,
give us hope
at your coming
so that we may be newly created
with you on Easter Day.

Mary Brogan

Tiberias, by Peter

We scurry shoreward under violet skies,
still laughing and expectant with a hope
outliving death.

The Master's love, companionship and prayer
now somehow buoy us up as if the Cross
has never stood.

But darkness, serge-like, subtly wraps itself
around this holy huddle in the boat.
We net no fish.

Soft dawnbreak looms assertively upon
the dim horizon, and a silhouette
is seen to speak

and heard to move, and longs to touch once more
the lives of friends by breaking bread and fish
and sharing life.

We take his point and drop the net, and strain
as undiscovered muscles petrify
and wait for death,

but Hope has gathered sticks and kindled fire
for Easter barbecue, as Love declares,
'It is the Lord'.

Those words resound most magically in me
as round unworthiness I wrap the cloak
of dignity,

and plunging with a holy joy now plumb
in faith the font of full Tiberias,
baptismally.

This is a day of echoes as the men,
the fish, the fishermen, fulfil his hopes
and flop to shore,

emerging weakly, panting for his love,
to pray for all the other pilgrim souls
in life's proud sea.

Already optimistic charcoal winks
and chuckles on the purifying fire,
enspiriting

for brave communion of bread and fish.
As once five thousand hopefuls had their fill
in serried ranks,

so now the starving faithful take their share,
feeding on the fruits of hope and faith,
though called to love.

Louise Swanston SSMN

John 21: 17

He said to him the third time, 'Simon, son of John, do you love
me?' Peter felt hurt because he said to him the third time, 'Do
you love me?' And he said to him, 'Lord, you know everything;
you know that I love you.' Jesus said to him, 'Feed my sheep.'

Tomb Day

It's a tomb day alright,
miserable and raining,
dreary and dull.
Bored, I go downstairs
to do my ironing
and think of Mary,
going back to
John's house
and getting on
with life.
On the outside,
nothing's changed,
but on the inside,
everything.
I think of her,
cooking, cleaning,
washing,
hanging out
the clothes
to dry
and
all the time
thinking,
wondering,
questioning,
remembering,
her son,
that once
was hers,
and

is

no
more.

Suzy Brouard

Mary's Remembering

Sometimes as I wander by the sea, near Magdala, I remember.
There is a lot to remember – the fishing boats, the call – my call
to follow.
And I did.
As the sea washes over my tired feet I remember that I poured my
soothing precious oil on his feet; my own offering, the best I had.
And he was glad, but Judas was angry, 'a waste' he said, he was so
keen on money for this and that and in the end he betrayed his
own friend.
Jesus was kind. . glad. He said what I had done would be
remembered.
Perhaps it will, perhaps it won't.
But what Jesus did WILL be remembered. He died on a cross and I
was there. No oil on his poor feet then, no men to be angry – just
we women, and John of course, staying to the end.
We watched him die,
we saw him laid to rest.
We were witnesses to his coming again.
But now I wander by the shore and think of all our feet have done.
The walking beside, the refreshing, the anointing, the pain and the
following. We have been forgotten for a while, but our feet and
our hearts march on.

Elizabeth Bradley (Rev.)

SECTION II

*Pentecost and
the work of the Spirit
in Ordinary Time*

Wisdom 7: 22–27, 8: 1

There is in her a spirit that is intelligent, holy,
unique, manifold, subtle,
mobile, clear, unpolluted,
distinct, invulnerable, loving the good, keen,
irresistible, beneficent, humane,
steadfast, sure, free from anxiety,
all-powerful, overseeing all,
and penetrating through all spirits
that are intelligent, pure and altogether subtle.

For wisdom is more mobile than any motion;
because of her pureness she pervades and penetrates all things.
For she is a breath of the power of God,
and a pure emanation of the glory of the Almighty;
therefore nothing defiled gains entrance in her.

For she is a reflection of eternal light,
a spotless mirror of the working of God,
and an image of his goodness.
Although she is but one, she can do all things,
and while remaining in herself, she renews all things

She reaches mightily from one end of the earth to the other,
and she orders all things well.

To the Holy Spirit

Let's not forget that you were never not.
Behind the broody storm's first turbulence
you hung, ingenious. You breathed, then blew
primeval waters into life, as underwing
you gathered noisy masterpiece of workshop's dawn.

Your tender shadow fathered fleshly Word
and mothered forth a Virgin's fearful Yes.
Gently the Creator formed and held the bulb that rocked,
lullabyed by fleeting Wind within the creases of Love's palm.
Trembling but safe in cooling air of Love's caress;
guarded, encircled, and urgent with the pulse of life,
corm forced a nod and strained
and yielded up her loud, eternal Shoot.

Small wonder Jordan's banks held back their breath
when God-with-Us proved faithful to his name
and donned humanity and bowed his head,
submerged in baptism beyond his need.
No marvel skies unlocked and you swept boldly down
and stirred stunned air and set your loyal seal
upon the Father's words, as on the Word's proud Father.
One-in-Three, you spelled out unity, endorsingly.

Down precious years you mothered miracles and fathered prayer;
huffed into life a love of truth and showed the world its God.
You breathed anonymous, behind the wings, waiting for cues
you never missed. You came, spoke out through mouths,
and came, rocking houses, breathing fire, arousing faith,
sustaining hope: the flaming Hand of God
plunging, sealing, lighting,
and freeing for a love that always burns.

A Master Craftsman played there by his side
and juggled many coloured balls and dreams.
Wade in now, playful Hoverer, and fold yourself
around this crying world.
South Wind, distil our yesterday and blow us on,
consoled and desolate,
encompassing tomorrow with a warm and dewy smile.

Louise Swanston SSMN

Proverbs 8: 24–30

When there were no depths I was brought forth,
    when there were no springs abounding with water.
Before the mountains had been shaped,
    before the hills, I was brought forth –
when he had not yet made earth and fields,
    or the world's first bits of soil.

When he established the heavens, I was there,
    when he drew a circle on the face of the deep,
when he made firm the skies above,
    when he established the fountains of the deep,
when he assigned to the sea its limit,
    so that the waters might not transgress his command,
when he marked out the foundations of the earth,
    then I was beside him, like a master worker.

Veni Creator Spiritus
Come Holy Ghost, Creator Come!

Come, be with us, for we are here to create,
to create, as Jesus witnessed women creating,
taking bushels of wheat, bushels of raw humanity
adding the yeast of their womanhood
working it in, kneading, kneading, labouring
to make it penetrate the substance of the raw wheat
to manufacture, to create the bread
that in turn will help to nourish, to sustain the life of the world.

We are here to create a new world:
a new world by our humble efforts,
in themselves as puny as those of the Jewish bakerwoman
whom we yet know as creatrix
in whom you have made visible your creative power.

Give us, Creator Spirit, a vision of the world
as your love would make it.
Help us to create a world where women are esteemed
and all the weak and poor appreciated.
Help us to create a world where the benefits of culture
are shared equally between men and women,
between races and nations.
Help us to create a world where peace is laced
with justice, and justice intertwined with love.

And help us, Creator supreme, to create a church
where all who share human life will recognise
in themselves and in others the one image of yourself
in which they were conceived.

Help us by the inspiration of your Spirit
to build this world – this church.

Amen   *Kira Sohldoost, rc*

Holy Spirit, grant me the WISDOM to remain calm
and just when disorder and panic move in.
Help me to have UNDERSTANDING so that I may
see the goodness in others when often
it is easier to condemn and criticise.
Show me how to give and keep COUNSEL
when tempers rise and threaten to steal my tolerance.
Infuse me with FORTITUDE that I will always have
the courage to stand up for my beliefs
however unfashionable or unpopular it makes me.
Inspire me with a KNOWLEDGE that is humble to give me
an insight into the needs of others
and those who suffer silently.
Develop a PIETY in my heart that is borne out of total
dependence and adoration of you alone.
May I always FEAR a separation from you through sin
and an awareness of your final judgement.
But above all, Lord make me fit and ready to receive the
gifts of your Holy Spirit and to use them for your glory.

AMEN

M Gough

Romans 15: 13

May the God of hope fill you with all joy
and peace in believing, so that you may
abound in hope by the power of the Holy Spirit

GOD, the source of hope...

Into our future God advances ahead of us.
That is what makes the future bearable, inviting,
full of possible meaning.
His presence in the future gives us hope.
For our life and the life of mankind He is preparing
something good –
not just a future which will happen,
but a future we can help to fashion
with Him and for Him.

Prayer

Lord God,
your word says you make all things new.
Give us such hope in you
that we become optimistic about everyone
    and everything else.
Lord of all hopefulness, Lord of the future,
lead us forward with a light step and a
    courageous heart;
to your honour and glory,
and for the sake of Jesus Christ,
your Son, and our Saviour.

Mair Bowen (Rev.)

we are gathered here
called together by the holy spirit,
the woman spirit of GOD
as she moves over the waters of creation
and over the earth;
we believe in the holy spirit, the woman spirit of GOD,
who like a mother hen created us
– gave us birth –
and covers us with her wings.
holy spirit, woman spirit of GOD, lead us from death to life,
from falsehood to truth;
lead us from despair to hope, and from fear to trust.
let light and peace fill our hearts,
our world,
our universe…
let us dream together,
work together,
to build together
one world of equality,
ONE WORLD OF PEACE AND JUSTICE FOR
ALL…
Amen

Kira Sohldoost, rc

Postscript to the sixteen Revelations of Divine Love (extract)

Our high Father, Almighty God, who is Being, He knoweth us and loveth us from before the beginning of time. Of this knowing, in His full, marvellous, deep charity, by the foreseeing endless counsel of all the blessed Trinity, He willed that the Second Person should become our Mother, our Brother and our Saviour. Wherefore it followeth that as truly as God is our Father so truly is God our Mother. Our Father willeth; our Mother worketh; our good Lord the Holy Ghost confirmeth. Therefore it belongeth to us to love our God, in whom we have our being, Him reverently thanking and praising for creating us, mightily praying to our Mother for mercy and pity, and to our Lord the Holy Ghost for help and grace.

Thus is Jesus our true Mother according to Nature, because He, being God, created us; and He is our true Mother according to Grace, by His taking of our created nature. All the fair working and all the sweet, kindly offices of dear-worthy Motherhood are appropriated to the Second Person, for in Him we have this goodly will whole and safe without end both by Nature and Grace, through His own proper goodness.

I understood three ways of beholding Motherhood in God. The first is grounded on His creation of our nature. The second is the taking of our nature – and there the Motherhood of Grace begins. The third is Motherhood of Working – in this is a forthspreading without end by the same Grace, in length and breadth, height and deepness. And all is one Love.

Julian of Norwich (translated by Anna Maria Reynolds CP)

Wisdom 7: 7–12

Therefore I prayed, and understanding was given me;
I called on God, and the spirit of wisdom came to me.
I preferred her to sceptres and thrones,
and I accounted wealth as nothing in comparison with her,
Neither did I liken to her any priceless gem,
because all gold is but a little sand in her sight,
and silver will be accounted as clay before her.
I loved her more than health and beauty,
and I chose to have her rather than light,
because her radiance never ceases.
All good things came to me along with her,
and in her hands uncounted wealth.
I rejoiced in them all, because wisdom leads them;
but I did not know that she was their mother.
I learned without guile and I impart without grudging;
I do not hide her wealth,
for it is an unfailing treasure for mortals;
those who get it obtain friendship with God,
commended for the gifts that come from instruction.

May God grant me to speak with judgement,
and to have thoughts worthy of what I have received;
for he is the guide even of wisdom
and the corrector of the wise.

2 Peter 3: 13–14

> But, in accordance with his promise, we wait for new heavens
> and a new earth, where righteousness is at home. Therefore,
> beloved, while you are waiting for these things, strive to be found
> by him at peace, without spot or blemish; and regard the
> patience of our Lord as salvation

Middle Time

Between the exhilaration of Beginning
And the satisfaction of Concluding
      is the Middle-time
of enduring – Changing... Trying
Despairing Continuing... Becoming.
Jesus Christ was the Person of God's Middle-time
Between Creation and... Accomplishment
    Through him God said of Creation
        "Without mistake"
        and of Accomplishment
        "Without doubt"

And we In our Middle-times
Of Wondering and Waiting
Hurrying and Hesitating
Regretting and Revising
      We who have begun many things
      and seen but few completed
      We who are becoming more and less

Through the evidence of God's Middle-Time
      Have a stabilising hint

That we are not mistakes
That we are irreplaceable
that our Being is of Interest
and our Doing is of purpose
that our Being and Doing
are surrounded by Amen.

Jesus Christ is the Completer
        of unfinished people
        with unfinished work
        in unfinished times

May he keep us from sinking, from ceasing
from wasting, from solidifying

        That we may be for him
        Experimenters, Enablers, Encouragers,
        and Associates in Accomplishment.

Lona Fowler

A letter to Mary

OUR LADY, During these past months I have thought so much about you expecting a baby and how hard that must have been for you when you were probably younger than our 16 year-old. When she quietly told me she was pregnant, she had already been offered, and turned down an abortion. She knew that life ought not to be destroyed. Yet in the age in which we live how much easier it would have been for her to take that option. Instead, she faced her friends and listened to those words, 'Why on earth are you having it? You must be mad.' In an age in which others seek careers, Christian motherhood remains a vocation. It was my daughter who reminded me of my own words to her: 'Motherhood is the most responsible job a person can be given.'

The expected birth is yet to be. Sixteen seems so young to be a parent. Meanwhile she faces GCSE exams. You never went to school; you learned at your mother's knee. Now I am teaching her at home. For these coming months we seek your prayers.

Work is not confined to school-work. There are shopping trips, the household routine and ante-natal care. No stones are thrown these days, except verbal ones; sometimes thrown by others of my generation who in blind ignorance fail to see the unknown story of many an abortion hidden within other adolescents who pass by them every day.

May your Son look kindly on our daughter and the countless other young, single mothers who she represents. Give to each one a deep devotion to her child, in spite of all the pressures and difficulties that lie ahead. May the parents of pregnant children give them the love and support they desperately need, and may their own painful and sorrowful feelings know your healing touch. May each person – baby, parent and grandparent – be open to the warmth of Divine Love and Compassion.

Mary we trust you. Pray for us all.

From a grandmother-to-be

Isaiah 66: 13–4

As a mother comforts her child,
   so will I comfort you;
   you shall be comforted in Jerusalem.
You shall see, and your heart shall rejoice;
your bodies shall flourish like the grass;
and it shall be known that the hand of
      the Lord is with his servants.

2 Corinthians 1: 3–4

Blessed be the God and Father of our Lord Jesus Christ, the Father of mercies and the God of all consolation, who consoles us in all our affliction, so that we may be able to console those who are in any affliction with the consolation with which we ourselves are consoled by God.

A Meditation

Creator God
you mothered me into being,
loving me into life.

Again and again
you pour your spirit through
my unsevered chord into my soul.
At my baptism you declared me
a 'beloved child'.
And now, each day, you hold me
carefully in the palm of your hand.

Again and again
as the listening mother
you hear my cries for help, nurse my hurts
and know my pain.

Again and again
you share my desolate feelings;
you soar with me in ecstatic moments.

Filled with compassion you always
welcome back this prodigal daughter.
So many times you tend my wounded heart.
In blackest times you simply…
                              carry your child.

Judy Gunthorpe

Isaiah 54: 10, 14

For the mountains may depart
   and the hills be removed,
but my steadfast love shall not depart from you,
and my covenant of peace shall not be removed,
says the Lord, who has compassion on you.

In righteousness you shall be established;
you shall be far from oppression,
   for you shall not fear;
and free from terror,
   for it shall not come near you.

But Jesus looked at them and said, "For mortals it is
impossible, but for God all things are possible" (Mt. 19: 26)

Ngora is expecting a baby. Her body is heavy with child; her face,
remote and thoughtful. A baby – that is something (someone)
wonderful: present and future incarnated in hopeful, darling flesh.
But Ngora is a refugee, and her baby is the consequence of rape,
back in that prison. Can life spring forth from such a death
experience? 'Nothing is impossible to God.'

Postscript

In March 1998, 'Ngora' (not her real name) gave birth to a fine,
healthy little boy. Since then, Ngora has been radiantly happy
and her face has become beautiful.
Truly – nothing is impossible to God.

Katharine Holmstrom SHCJ

Ecclesiastes 3: 1–8

For everything there is a season, and
a time for every matter under heaven:
a time to be born, and a time to die;
a time to plant, and a time to pluck up what is planted;
a time to kill, and a time to heal;
a time to break down, and a time to build up;
a time to weep, and a time to laugh;
a time to mourn, and a time to dance;
a time to throw away stones, and
a time to gather stones together;
a time to embrace, and
a time to refrain from embracing;
a time to seek, and a time to lose;
a time to keep, and a time to throw away;
a time to tear, and a time to sew;
a time to keep silent, and a time to speak;
a time to love, and a time to hate;
a time for war, and a time for peace.

Now is a time for planting

In me is a field:
Sometimes in harvest,
Sometimes in winter.
And God's hands may
overturn the soil,
digging deep,
or she may brush
her finger-tips, lightly,
over the top of the earth.

But recently
the field has been barren,
And the seeds apparently
dormant.
But has God been
ploughing the soil, gently,
both by day and by night,
I wonder?

Yes; I wonder if I am
ready
for this God,
who has cleared the land
And planted, not corn,
but Oak trees.

For though
my voice is silent now,
soon it will be LOUD.

But now is a time for planting.

Suzy Brouard

Talking of God

A woman's hands to knead His bread,
A woman's hair to dry His feet,
A woman's voice to tell of His mystery.
Mary's voice to sing of His mystery.

Was God's great love to half the world denied?
Did Mary quake for fear of speaking?
Men held the books which left women untried,
But women hold now the language men are
seeking.

Hearts and minds communing now,
Rivers and streams and seas revealing
The unifying Word being spoken on earth.

Women and men assuming now
Wings of the Spirit, soaring, gleaming,
Freely sharing their joyful rebirth.

Word and flesh and spirit enshrined,
Voices of women and men combine
To sing God's song, for humankind

Maggie Jackson

Galatians 3: 23–29

Now before faith came, we were imprisoned and guarded under the law until faith would be revealed. Therefore the law was our disciplinarian until Christ came, so that we might be justified by faith. But now that faith has come, we are no longer subject to a disciplinarian, for in Christ Jesus you are all children of God through faith. As many of you as were baptised into Christ have clothed yourselves with Christ. There is no longer Jew or Greek, there is no longer slave or free, there is no longer male or female; for all of you are one in Christ Jesus. And if you belong to Christ, then you are Abraham's offspring, heirs according to the promise.

For Forgiveness

Sorrowing God, we bring before you the pain and failure in our lives…
The times when we are hurt, or lash out at others.
When grief, misery or doubt overwhelm us and block out everything
    else
When we feel frustrated, hungry or ill and unable to take control of
    our lives.
When we feel paralysed by anger or resentment.
The times when we feel isolated from others who know what is
    going on.
When we ourselves raise barriers to show that we belong,
but only end up excluding people.

Lord, we bring before you our lives
We lay them before you with sorrow and ask for your healing.

Rachel Lampard and Jennie Richmond (CHAS)

Isaiah 58: 9–10

Then you shall call, and the Lord will answer;
you shall cry for help, and he will say, Here I am.

If you remove the yoke from among you,
the pointing of the finger, the speaking of evil,
if you offer your food to the hungry
and satisfy the needs of the afflicted,
then your light shall rise in the darkness
and your gloom be like the noonday.

Life Loom

accept the offering of ourselves
women and men... men and women
our separate strands,
to be woven in and out
over and under and through
as we seek to become together
the strands...
men and women... women and men
a part of life
a part of church
A PART OF YOU

give us a vision of the tapestry you weave...
with our willingness to be shuttled back and forth,
women and men... men and women... back and forth...
as the tapestry of days becomes the tapestry of years,
but the vision of tapestries remain...
the patterns and the fabric that COULD be, that could be,
as we are shuttled back and forth... men and women...
women and men... back and forth... the strands out of which
you weave a fabric... a tapestry... OF LIFE... OF CHURCH...
OF YOU...
amen

Kira Sohldoost, rc

The Journey

"Come, let us go up
to the mountain
of the Lord,
to the house of
the God of Jacob;
that he may teach
us his ways
and that we may walk
in his paths"

Isaiah 2: 3

1 How can I come close to you?
I want to be your friend,
to be befriended.
I want, you know I do,
to reach out for your hand.

But there is a block
I need to pass beyond.
Before my first faltering move,
I learn the truth, the shock.
I'm as in a quicksand.

It is myself impedes.
I struggle to remove my own-disgust,
self-love, unfreedom, pride.
Held down by worldly needs,
what am I to do?

Forget the past. Christ died – you say.
This inchoate experience of you
is changing me from what I am
to that I am. You say – just pray
and search my being anew.

2 I no longer want; now long,
for you are showing me
the mantra for my life,
not self, but love alone.
What am I to do?

The darkness of unknowing frightens me;
such darkness only shafts of love can pierce.
You say – completely lose myself.
Come stark, in all humility,
to feel, not see, the path ahead.

Still, self is strong.
To see, the ultimate in being, is my all.
Help me to change from that I am
to I am as I am. For you I long
but the sierra ahead is hard to tread.

Once in sharing human love
I sensed my inner self, the depth of being.
But you ask more. I must be most myself.
Give me the strength to stretch above,
outside my human vision.

3 No longer to the law of love be meek;
now utterly submit to love's great, guiding power;
go beyond seeing you, Creator, in those around.
More is needed to achieve the peak.
You brook no division.

In you, the cosmic creator of all,
I am to love all people, all that is,
all the wonders of the universe.
This… is your call.
I know now what to do !

But in the doing?

I will go on, my friend.

With your spirit I can achieve
what by nature is beyond.
The clouds of darkness will be swept away.
My faith is strong and I believe !
Lord, love incarnate, help my unbelief.

Petal Mary O'Hea

Psalm 27: 1, 5, 9, 13, 14

The Lord is my light and my salvation;
    whom shall I fear?
The Lord is the stronghold of my life;
    of whom shall I be afraid?

For he will hide me in his shelter
    in the day of trouble;
he will conceal me under the cover of his tent;
    he will set me high on a rock

Do not turn your servant away in anger,
    you who have been my help.
Do not cast me off, do not forsake me,
    O God of my salvation!
If my father and my mother forsake me,
    the Lord will take me up.

I believe that I shall see the goodness of the Lord
    in the land of the living.
Wait for the Lord;
    be strong, and let your heart take courage;
wait for the Lord!

Where are You in the Time of Our Troubles?

How can we believe in you, God, when we have to live
       in uncertainty:
How can we trust you when we see the smoke rising from
       the volcano?
Women worry for the future of their children,
       men anguish over the harvests which may not be.
Children cling to their parents for fear of the dark.

Where is your saving hand, O God?
Where is your kindness and pity?

When hardship and fear abound, you are there in those
       who listen and take the strain.
Sharing and hospitality, self-denial and benevolence are
       the signs of your presence.
These will always be with us when you are with us, these
       will always remain as long as your love remains.

Where are you, God, in the time of our troubles?
You are always with us in the good times and the bad.
You are always with us

Janice Clark

Come Follow Me?

Come follow me
Who? Me?
Yes you
Why? Why me?

Rosa, come follow me
Rosa, he said Rosa
He called me by my name
MY NAME

What is my name?
A Rose
A Rose, a perfect flower,
beautiful, perfumed, cultivated,
thornless
on a long, slender stem.
A Rose, my name
He called me by MY NAME

No, that is not my name
More of a wild rose.
A faded rose
the last rose of summer
A rose in a garden of weeds
Prickly, hurtful
Not much to offer
He can't mean me

Come, follow me,
COME FOLLOW ME
Who? Me ?
Yes, Come follow me.
Why ? Why me ?

I need you, I want you, I LOVE
YOU,
Even me ?
Yes, you. Come follow me
Yes, Lord, I am coming,
Come follow me. Yes Lord –
Show me – how ?
I am coming

Rosa

Lord, let me be the one that is yet to be in Spirit and in Truth

Let my hands be your hands
Let me say YES without fear and follow you.
Lead me where I would not choose to go –
    rest is for later, let me jump in.
I choose redemption and creation.
Fear of what may be has no place in the NOW

Ladies of Lancaster group

Resting Place

There she lies
Knees pulled up to her chest
Eyes tightly shut
Cushioned by darkness
Hidden from the world.

She is perfection
Perfect hands
Perfect feet
Perfect brain, untarnished by knowledge
Her mother's pride and joy.

"We so wanted a baby",
Said the father to the reporter
Who was there at the scene
When the mother was found
Stone cold by the roadside.

"Hit and run" said the coroner,
"Died instantly", said the doctor,
"Amen" said the vicar,
As she was lowered into her grave.

Knees pulled up to her chest
Eyes tightly shut
Cushioned by darkness   *Emma Katherine Poulter*
Hidden from the world.   (a 19 year old student)

Psalm 25: 16–18

Turn to me and be gracious to me,
for I am lonely and afflicted.
Relieve the troubles of my heart,
and bring me out of my distress.
Consider my affliction and my trouble,
and forgive all my sins.

Love in Motion

Sometimes we only listen
Sometimes we are just there
Sometimes someone is reaching out
Because they need to share.

Then a miracle is taking place
Invisible to see
For when we reach and touch someone
We set that person free.

We open up the bolted door
We find the hidden key
Just by being patient
We let that person be.

For love that is in motion
Given freely with no strings
Helps the wounded heart be blessed
By the healing that it brings.

J. Scott

Ecclesiasticus 6: 14–16

Faithful friends are a sturdy shelter:
whoever finds one has found a treasure.
Faithful friends are beyond price;
no amount can balance their worth.
Faithful friends are life-saving medicine;
and those who fear the Lord will find them.

A Mother's Prayer

And now in turn I bear a son,
And tenderly I set him free.
Then day by day I see him do
to me, what I have done to You.

I may not have his need for drugs,
Nor live my life alone and scared.
But I do know the doubt and fear,
Those deepest thoughts I've never shared.

As my weak will reflects in his,
His need for help is my need too.
Yet he withdraws to useless dreams
Whereas I simply turn to You.

I realise Your boundless love;
Your tender heart, where mine is stone.
I can't forgive as You forgive
and yet you call me still, your own.

Hold my poor son within your hands
And gently stroke his ravaged face.
Love him for me, I pray this night
And fill him with your healing grace.
                    Amen

Judy Gunthorpe

Prayer

I know that when the stress has grown too strong
    Thou wilt be there
I know that when the waiting seems so long
    Thou hearest prayer
I know that through the crash of falling worlds
    Thou holdest me
I know that life and death and all are Thine
    Eternally

Janet Stuart RSCJ (1914–1957)

Isaiah 42: 1–3, 16

Here is my servant, whom I uphold,
    my chosen, in whom my soul delights;
I have put my spirit upon him;
    he will bring forth justice to the nations.

He will not cry out or lift up his voice,
    or make it heard in the street;
a bruised reed he will not break,
    and a dimly burning wick he will not quench;
    he will faithfully bring forth justice.

I will lead the blind by a road they do not know,
by paths they have not known I will guide them.
I will turn the darkness before them into light,
    the rough places into level ground.
These are the things I will do,
    and I will not forsake them.

Why they came

To worship and sing
near stone pillars and
stained glass windows
in silent prayer
That's why they were there

Some people came in to view
the art and carved wood
and ponder was it good

Other folk dashed in
out of the rain,
the Cathedral dome
a home

I'm sure God knows why
each one came.

Mavis Catlow

Psalm 139: 1–6, 8–10

O Lord, you have searched me and known me.
You know when I sit down and when I rise up;
you discern my thoughts from far away.
You search out my path and my lying down,
and are acquainted with all my ways.

Even before a word is on my tongue,
      O Lord, you know it completely.
You hem me in, behind and before,
      and lay your hand upon me.
Such knowledge is too wonderful for me;
      it is so high that I cannot attain it.

If I ascend to heaven, you are there;
      if I make my bed in Sheol, you are there.
If I take the wings of the morning
      and settle at the farthest limits of the sea,
even there your hand shall lead me,
      and your right hand shall hold me fast.

Sheol = Hebrew for the place where the dead continue to exist underground

Longing

I have no picture of what I've lost
There is nothing to show
No visible scars
My mantelpiece shows no photos of my children
That I could show and then you would understand
My pain.

My mantelpiece is empty
There are no children to show you
There is no pain that you could see
My photos are in my head
Dreams of what my children would be.

But my dreams are broken
And my heart aches with disappointment
My eyes cry with grief
My heart hoped once, that my dreams would come true
Like a fairytale
But my hope is gone
I lost that too somewhere
And still the blood and pain come
As a reminder of what can be
If my fairytale came true.

Paula

(Note – this was written after Paula was told that
she could not have children)

Unexpected Treasure

Hope is given as a gift
Unexpectedly
A small seed implanted
A treasure
Giving strength to face each new day
Hope is life giving
A small flicker of light in darkness
That if it goes unhindered
Will grow to a shining brilliance
And from hope will flow
Life, expectancy, joy, love
Life begins with hope.

Hope needs nurture to survive
And a dark place to grow
Nourishment to fan the flame
Divine love
That is soft, fluid, transparent
That soothes and coaxes the flame
To shine brightly
And thus welcoming love into it's home
The ultimate treasure.

Paula

(Note – this was written later after the birth of Paula's first child)

Mary

O give me a statue of Mary the Worker
skirts hitched above dust-covered feet;
first century Palestinian apron
interestingly splashed; sleeves rolled up;
brown arms always ready to fetch water;
workaday veil fixed back; and dark hair
curling round happy dark brown eyes.

Is she singing a psalm, laughing with friends,
or tickled at some antic of her Son?

That's a person I'd believe, love.

Olive Powell

Joseph: The Hidden the Silent

We know so little of him from the Gospels. Yet he was chosen by God, to have the important role of providing a name, a home, a family and a haven for Mary and her child Jesus.

He was

Silent
Strong
Honourable
Obedient
Caring
Responsible
Self sacrificing
Hardworking
Responsive
Religious
Challenging
and finally Absent –
so Silent once more.

We too, are chosen, with important and yet perhaps hidden roles.

May we emulate his qualities to be a quiet presence for good in the world.

Janet Ward

Hope

When Jesus was presented in the Temple as a baby, the old man, Simeon, took him in his arms and felt there the potential hope for mankind, not in terms of success or comfort for the baby's mother but as a 'light to lighten the Gentiles'.

I believe this to be still true. Although cautious myself in my ideas about a future life, I have become convinced that "Faith gives substance to our hopes and makes us certain of realities we do not see" (Hebrews, 11:1).

It may be hard to be hopeful in times of despair, but the concentration of thought upon just one example of love can be helpful. Anthony Grey in his book 'Hostage in Peking', describes how he tried to combat hopelessness during his solitary confinement by renaming the days of the week:

Wednesday was the Day of Hope; Thursday was the Day of Expectancy. A message of hope is still an essential part of Quakerism, especially as our form of worship is based on expectancy. Paul lived in times of great cruelty; he was lonely, often depressed, imprisoned and persecuted, yet he could write words which have meaning for us today:

"...hope is no mockery, because God's love has flooded our inmost heart through the Holy Spirit he has given us" (Romans 5: 5)

Dorothy Webster (1916–1975)

John 4: 14

"Those who drink of the water that I will give them will never be thirsty. The water that I will give will become in them a spring of water gushing up to eternal life"

The Woman at the Well

Living Water
> Bubbling within me for eternal life
>> Peace
>>> A smile
>>>> Sun glinting on the ripples.

Living water

The old me, sneaking to the well
> At siesta time, when nobody would see me;

A stranger chatting me up,
> Giving new answers to provocative questions.
>> Truth shining through every chink
>> Till the armour tumbled

And I, the outcast, ran to face my neighbours
> With dazzling news.

There was no miracle here,
> Only the real miracle of truth:

Jew and Samaritan hearing the good news together,
> Jew and Samaritan sharing food,

Enjoying a two-day visit, friendship, not hatred.

Now the village says: "We have heard him for ourselves now",
And I smile, brimming with living water.
"We don't just believe because of what you told us."
I smile.We all share the same truth.
> We met him. We know
>> The Saviour of the world is among us.

We hear the news from Judea,
> We rejoice or we worry,
We shake our heads:
> "What will they do with him?"
Will they welcome the truth?

Truth that has set me free
To face myself, to be myself
To trust
> God's presence.
>> Living water.

F. Mary Callan

The Call

Called to listen, and in the listening to hear.
Called to hear, and in the hearing to follow.
Called to follow, and in the following to die.
Called to die, and in the dying to live.
Called to live, and in the living to love.
Called to love, and in the loving to be loved.
Called to become ONE.

Ladies of Lancaster group

Isaiah 43: 6–10

"Do not withhold;
bring my sons from far away
and my daughters from the end of the earth –
everyone who is called by my name,
whom I created for my glory
whom I formed and made."

Bring forth the people who are blind,
yet have eyes,
who are deaf, yet have ears!
Let all the nations gather together
and let the peoples assemble.
Who among them declared this,
and foretold to us the former things?
Let them bring their witnesses to justify them,
and let them hear and say, "It is true."
You are my witnesses, says the Lord,
and my servant whom I have chosen,
so that you may know and believe me
and understand that I am he.

In the name of the Father
    who gave me life,
and of the Son
    who shows me life,
and of the Holy Spirit
    who empowers my life;

I approach this day with
    hope in your guidance.
I embrace this day with
    faith in your goodness.
I offer this day with
    love in my heart.

    Let this be truly true!

    Amen.

Rosemary Murphy

Psalm 9: 1–2, 7–8

I will give thanks to the Lord with my whole heart;
I will tell of all your wonderful deeds.
I will be glad and exult in you;
    I will sing praise to your name, O Most High

But the Lord sits enthroned for ever,
    he has established his throne for judgement.
He judges the world with righteousness;
    he judges the peoples with equity.

The Response

What it is – What is it
You're calling me again
How many times has this call come in my life?
What is it you really want of me Lord?
And am I really ready to give?
Give What? – Time, Energy, Love, Service... So the list goes on.
The excitement rushes and the challenge grows.
This time Lord – this time. I'll try, I'll try
But always in the sure knowledge That when I fail once again
You'll pick me up and carry me... until The Next Time.

Ladies of Lancaster group

Isaiah 43: 1–3

But now thus says the Lord,
   he who created you, O Jacob,
   he who formed you, O Israel:
Do not fear, for I have redeemed you;
   I have called you by name,
      you are mine.
When you pass through the waters,
      I will be with you;
and through the rivers,
      they shall not overwhelm you;
  when you walk through the fire
      you shall not be burned,
and the flame shall not consume you.
For I am the Lord your God,
   the Holy One of Israel, your Saviour.
I give Egypt as your ransom,
   Ethiopia and Seba in exchange for you.

Litany of the Ladies of Lancaster

Jesus asks Who do you think I am?
To me you are:
Loving friend
Loving Father
The bringer of the good news of the kingdom, light and guide.
You are the one who tolerates, who forgives,
You are the centre of my life, the core of my being.
LOVE
MY LIFE
A comfort but also my greatest challenge, my saviour and comforter.
  Loving Master-King of the universe pure love and light and colour
My inspiration and guide: the one who believes in me
My hope and my light
My Lord, My God, My Saviour.
Jesus, My Guide, Strength and Comfort.

Ephesians 4: 1–6

I therefore, the prisoner in the Lord, beg you to lead a life worthy of the calling to which you have been called, with all humility and gentleness, with patience, bearing with one another in love, making every effort to maintain the unity of the Spirit in the bond of peace. There is one body and one Spirit, just as you were called to the one hope of your calling, one Lord, one faith, one baptism, one God and Father of all, who is above all and through all and with all.

"Send forth Your Spirit and we shall be created and You will renew the face of the earth" We are all familiar with this prayer which describes the two-fold action of the Spirit in giving His gifts and calling into ministry. Firstly, we ourselves are re-created and transformed, made holy; and secondly, the ministries He calls us to are calls to service, to renew both the Church and the world. These two dimensions of the Spirit's action are inseparable, you cannot have one without the other. Only as we grow in holiness, in other words more like Jesus, will our ministries be effective and fruitful. In fact, without the Spirit's gifts we would be as useless as 'booming gongs or clashing cymbals,' and the needs and critical challenges of our century would overwhelm us; indeed the Spirit's power is as necessary to us today as it was to the early Church.

To minister is to serve, to be called and empowered by the Spirit, and this applies equally to the humblest, most hidden form of service as to the most public. It is important that all those already serving in their various capacities in the Church recognise this. Similarly, it is important for the rest of the Body of Christ to love and support them. In addition it is vital for every person to ask God to show him or her their particular ministry. There are no exceptions to ministry: ALL are called. Unity in service is a sure sign of the presence and activity of the Spirit and St Paul reminds us that as different parts of the one community, it is together that we, *"form a single body because we all have a share in this one loaf (the Eucharist)"*.
(1 Corinthians 1: 10–17)

Sue Norris

The Parable of the Talents

The parable can be seen as fundamentally about what each one of us does with the gifts God has given us at birth. All of us are born in God's image and likeness; this means we have a huge potential investment available for use in our lives.

What I have found encouraging about this parable is the notion of using and developing the talents with which God blessed me; especially as the ones I identified in myself as a teenager were not considered conventional for a girl. I remember a sense of isolation and sadness, almost despair, when I realised that what I was good at was not shared by other girls around me. After quite a long period of time, encouragement came to me from this parable; if what I was studying was where I had potential because God had given it to me then surely I was on the right track in continuing in those studies.

Increasing familiarity with the story led me to think further. The successful servants were given their rewards in the form of greater responsibilities. The paradox is that the return from using one's gifts from God can lie in the requirement to work a bit harder! But is work always only hard and uncomfortable? Some of it certainly is, for all of us, but let us not forget that succeeding in an activity, an investment of one's personal skill, can be very rewarding and greatly enjoyable. The real reward is that, in discovering what are one's particular gifts from God, there lies a great deal of satisfaction, pleasure and enjoyment.This might be termed 'fun'! Let's have more of that! Surely God meant us to have fun when we can.

Anne Leeming

(From: Women of the New Testament, N.B.C.W. 1997)

Scraps: The Presence of God (Feeding of the 5,000)

Amid the breadcrusts and the fish-bones
I sit in bliss, glorying in this moment,
Fed by the Messiah.

Below me, the murmur of voices:
The disciples get organised to pick up the scraps.
The fading light, the dwindling crowd,
The distant bustle,
The food, from nowhere, that has filled me.
The generosity, the permanence of God's gift,
shown by the scraps littering the landscape,
        Twelve hampers full!
The seagulls wheel and squawk,
Strut and gorge themselves among the leftovers.
        Bonanza for them !
God loves us !
Here, among the scraps, He loves us

F. Mary Callan

Matthew 14: 16–20

Jesus said to them, "They need not go away; you give them
something to eat". They replied, "We have nothing here but five
loaves and two fish". And he said, "Bring them here to me". Then
he ordered the crowds to sit down on the grass. Taking the five
loaves and the two fish, he looked up to heaven, and blessed and
broke the loaves, and gave them to the disciples, and the
disciples gave them to the crowds. And all ate and were filled.

The Excluded

> The Lord is near to the broken-hearted
> and saves the crushed in spirit.
> *Psalm 34: 18*

The excluded. Who are they? They are the people we don't
like to think about too much. We walk past them in the street
as they huddle in doorways. They are the people who have
nothing, at a time when conspicuous consumption is everything.

But we should never forget that Jesus was born in the poorest
surroundings, to an unmarried mother, and spent his life as an
itinerant preacher. Have we built up so many barriers in our
world that we are too afraid to go outside to meet him? We
pray for open hearts and open minds, we pray that we may
learn to make room for everyone and turn no one away.

Linda Jones (CAFOD)

Temple Cleansing

Sometimes, the only right response is
Anger. Not dull resentment,
Poisoning all it touches, or
Bitterness that taints the memory,
But a clean, cutting edge that
Lances festering grievances.
Releasing energy to fight;
The fuel of passion that
Challenges evils,
Outwardly observed
Or known within.
Such anger is not sin.

Ann Lewin

Pat is only one of many people I visit
But I go as often as I can
Don't hear me as some angel
I need to visit her for me!
I think I'm her number one Fan!
Escaping from the 'crash, bang, wallop'
Of the cruel world outside
I relax and regenerate,
In her quiet room I hide
In that Cheshire home for the very ill
My friend has come to terms
With her raw deal in life
She has – as we should – learned
To count her blessings, however sparse
She can make me feel ashamed
Has no idea of this lesson she's taught
My dear friend, so crippled and lamed
This – the true story of LOVE!

Mary Armstrong

Lord, when we walk away from our problems, meet us on the road;
when we are dejected and alone, bring us the joy of your
companionship, that we may carry the power of resurrection
into a dead and despairing world.

Susan Williams

Mary Immaculate

with your swift and simple response
to the Angel of the Annunciation,
you opened yourself wholly
to the life-giving action of the Spirit,
and became the Mother of our Saviour.

You followed where the Spirit led,
even to the foot of the Cross;
and you were at the heart of the mission of the Church
on the day of Pentecost.

Intercede for us,
that we may walk in attentiveness to the same Spirit;
that we may follow wherever he leads us;
and that, in simplicity and boldness,
we may always witness to his inexhaustible love

Mary, Woman of the Holy Spirit, pray for us

Ruth Duckworth DHS (1916–1996)

Enduring to the End

"But anyone who endures to the end will be saved" (Matthew 24: 13)

Whatever we are given to endure, be it darkness or merely twilight, the Lord will, at the end of time, return in a brilliance which will illuminate all things. Then, if we have abandoned our spark of divine fire and become one with the gloom, this light of Christ will be an unbearable intrusion. But if there is still a glow within us, we will leap for joy at his coming to rekindle our flame, and we will become truly one with the eternal divine light.

If we only allow the Holy Spirit, the divine wind, to fan our spark of fire, we will keep it aflame ready for Christ's Second Coming.

Gillian Crow

The Holy Family

The feast of the Holy Family is celebrated on the first Sunday after Christmas. We pray, 'to live as the Holy Family united in love'.

Sometimes it is hard for us to relate to the model of the Holy Family so often depicted: the calm serene parents, the docile child, difficulty and conflict absent, simply passive undemanding love. What has this to do with family life as we experience it?

When we look beneath the saccharine images we see something different: a frightened girl, pregnant and unmarried; a man whose first reaction was to put Mary aside; a couple ostensibly married, but with no sexual relationship and no other children.

Nor was the child Jesus a comfortable presence. After the shocking start of Mary's pregnancy, unforeseen journeys become necessary to Judea, to Bethlehem, and later to Egypt and Jerusalem. Unexpected strangers appeared at his birth. Disconcerting things were said by angels in strange dreams, and by people like Simeon and Anna in the Temple. We know that Jesus himself was direct and challenging and unintentionally hurtful to his parents. As an adult he could be angry, rebuke others, and express strong feelings. He was fully human.

When we attempt to project our limited ideas onto the real family of Joseph, Mary and Jesus we fail, they do not fit; they deny the humanity of this family, of any family, which involves the pain of being human, and the suffering which change demands.
We recognise the demands which love makes. We acknowledge our brokenness, our suffering, our pain, our need to change, our need to love and be loved.

We pray to live as the Holy Family, as a community of love, the love which can lead us to true holiness and peace.

Janet Ward

Litany

Mary, you responded to God's request, pray that we too may accept
    his call
Mary, homeless at Christ's birth, pray for those without a home
Mary, unmarried mother, pray for single parents
Mary, refugee in Egypt, pray for asylum seekers
Mary, mother of Jesus, pray for our daughters and our sons
Mary, living in poverty, pray for the deprived
Mary, standing by the cross, pray that we remain faithful to Jesus
Mary, embracing your dead son, pray for us at the hour of our death
Mary, rejoicing in your risen son, pray that we may rise with him
Mary, first apostle, pray for all who spread the Good News

NBCW Ecumenical Committee

SECTION III

Advent, Incarnation, Reconciliation and the coming of the Kingdom

HE LIVED
AMONG US
AND WE SAW
HIS GLORY

something
we have
watched
and touched
with our
own hands

Dear Lord,
As we approach the Millennium and anniversary of your
birth into this world may we receive you with a little of the
sense of wonder and the humility of Mary. Grant that more
may come to believe so that when you return to earth a great
people will throng from every corner to greet you. Amen.

Patricia Weitz

Romans 8: 18–24

I consider that the sufferings of this present time
are not worth comparing with the glory about
to be revealed to us. For the creation waits
with eager longing for the revealing of the children
of God; for the creation was subjected to futility,
not of its own will but by the will of the one who
subjected it, in hope that the creation itself will
be set free from its bondage to decay and will
obtain the freedom of the glory of the children of
God. We know that the whole creation has
been groaning in labour pains until now; and not
only the creation, but we ourselves, who have the
first fruits of the Spirit, groan inwardly while we
wait for adoption, the redemption of our
bodies. For in hope we were saved.

Advent

Waiting, waiting in silent stillness,
Pondering the Word of God in her heart
She listens in attentive willingness
To His Word that in speaking, acts.

Joy in patiently waiting on God
That He will come is as sure as the dawn
Each moment is a fresh coming
Be ready in quiet contemplation
amidst all the turmoil and rush.

Be right in the heart of your living each day
He is there to be heard and be seen.
As He speaks, so He acts, for to Him both are One,
And He'll do more than we could ever dream.

Martine Patoir

Prayer

Do we not think that Mary spent her time
spinning soft wool and weaving small clothes
in loving preparation for His coming?

May we too, who also use our time
spinning mere words and weaving them all
          into sentences
await His coming with the same love.

Mary Brogan

Incarnation

Stillness.
Eternity
hushed waiting.
God's frailty held
in human freedom:
"I am your handmaid –
be it unto me according to Your Word."
Her
"Yes"
united
echoing
the pulsating heartbeat
in
God
Eternal.
Glory
comes
unto His own.
Veiled
humble
Love
poured out
in
tiny being.
Life leaping to life.
Joy and Wonder
in Mary's womb.
Light into darkness comes.
The Divine 'Yes'
reconciling all creation
through and for Himself.

A. J. Hull

I have shed so many tears for the emptiness within me
Felt unbearable pangs of longing for having my own baby.
It's harder still when other women, pregnant, share their news.
I crave to rid me of my barrenness, to step out of these empty shoes.

A child is the ultimate seed of love, giving reason to live and to hope,
Without which, life seems so pointless... there is no need to cope.
As my spirit languishes I grow old with an esteem of lowly worth,
Void of the completeness sensed when one's child is given birth.

Yet, should such sadness and despair be allowed to take a hold
When God has given us his only son, a gift more precious than gold.
It was Mary who bore the Christ Child; on my behalf she suffered
The pains of labour, the fears and joys known well by all who've
mothered.

So let joy replace my sorrows at the approach of Christmas time,
As, after many years of heartache, I expect now a child sublime.
No more do I house an emptiness of unmeasurable dimensions,
Now all my redundant love within abounds freely without tensions.

With awe, anticipation and excitement I prepare
To greet this God-sent baby which all, with me, will share.
He will fill that painful emptiness with love and hope and joys.
All that! ...A wondrous gift!... Let all the world rejoice.

Pauline Coulson

"Comfort my people, comfort, it is God who speaks…"

How, God, are we your people
Save by the faithfulness of heart
that clings to the truth of your
      Being
being for us.

Comfort abounds around us:
in the mellow haze of drink,
the sharp shot of drugs
cutting out the empty longing
      our sad lives hold.

A God who longs to comfort us
      we who are his people;
who gives us freedom and loves us well
      Leaves to us the task of seeing
that in this emptiness lies
      his saving Love.

      Emmanuel
    God is truly with us.

Anne Hine, rscj

Gift to Our World

Child of our world
Born into all time, Two thousand years ago.
By Mary's yes
God's will, in Spirit's overshadowing
Made flesh and bone
Of Word which all created things began.
Where are You now
Amid this earth's noise and egocentric bustling?

Boy of our world
Growing for all time, Two thousand years ago.
Skilled at the lathe, Teaching in Temple, example of living.
Mary and Joseph
Loving and training safe home at Nazareth.
Where are You now
When marriage is doubted family crumbling?

Man of our world
Leading for all time, Two thousand years ago.
Walking on water
Curing the injured, restoring to life.
Welcomed with Palms
Condemned, Thorn crowned and Crucified.
Where are You now
As decadence, distress and discord are rife?

King of our world
Ascended to Heaven, Spirit despatching.
Teaching continues
Throughout all ages, Peoples shall hear You.
Celebrate Jubilee
Freedom to captives, Justice Sharing Hope Peace.
You are here now
Your love in creation to make all things new.

Janette Woodford, 1998 ©

Advent Prayers

The commercial Christmas, Lord – it's a bit much. It's hard to find
You in these milling crowds. But wait a minute! You fed crowds with
bread and fishes; You talked to crowds of the Father's love. Lord,
help me to speak a blessing on all the shovers and pushers today –
even when they tread on my toes.

The crib... The figures are in place, Lord – the baby in his terra cotta
feeding trough, the adoring mother, the watchful husband, the
kneeling shepherds.
And the kings have started their long journey to You via the
bedroom window sill, the bathroom shelf and the bookcases – a
perilous trek!
Assist me, Lord, in all the dangers of my pilgrim way – through the
turmoil of daily living, bring me to the stillness of the stable, and the
baby of Bethlehem.

Dawn Williams

Wisdom 18: 14–15

For while gentle silence enveloped all
    things,
and night in its swift course was now
    half gone,
your all-powerful word leapt from
    heaven, from the royal throne,
into the midst of the land that was
    doomed

Welcome the Lord !

He'll come! He's coming! Prepare the way,
Make space for the Messiah !
Throw out all rubbish, clutter, stuffing, stuff, encumbrance:
Be naked, free – and joyful !
Raise your heads, look up and glimpse
The spring, the springtime of the world, the Birth…
The longing of the nations
Murmurs, hums, swells and rises to a cry,
The anguished, ardent cry of people, hungry people,
A People in distress
An expectation. Rejoice, be comforted
The Shepherd-King is on his way!
Hearken, ye watchers: leap up
And stretch your hands to heaven.
Welcome the One who comes,
Who comes to liberate his dear ones.

He cannot bear to tarry longer.
He must needs burst his bonds and swoop
Upon us, gathering his chicks, his sheep, upon his heart.
Break forth into our world, Lord. Conquer and sanctify !
Invade our weakling planet,
Our chasm of misery, sordid mess:
Baptise us in your fire –
Burn, drown, transform and glorify.
Roar your purifying wind among, throughout, within us !
Capsize our wispy, strawlike dreams and feeble intentions
Into the ocean of your power and greatness,
Whirlpool of eternal wonder.
Cauterize and heal our many wounds, our gaping sores,
Our sinfulness. We know not what we do.
Have mercy! Pour out upon our humbled heads
No fire of punishment (though merited),
But oil of love, forgiveness.
All we, like sheep, have gone astray.
All we, together, sin, get up, and sin again:
Feckless, blind, ungrateful, rendering not
The glory of holiness due in justice to
The King of Kings, the living, Risen Saviour.
So: come, Lord ! Make haste, bright Sun of justice!
Sing, rise up, bound towards us, good Jesus:
Your dear and sorry world awaits you… Come !

Katharine Holmstrom SHCJ

Advent Thoughts from Our Lady in Old Age

Come my dearest, come –
Here from before all time,
And here in time,
And gone from me,
While ever with me, –
Come.

Before the Father made this world –
Before the Spirit's breath
Moved on those waters:
Before light came,
You were.

Alive and active
You the Word –
The Word He spoke
And promise that He gave,
To send and save;
To make us His: or rather
Make us own that we are His.

So coming from eternity to time,
While never leaving Him,
You came to me –
His handmaid. Who am I
That I should mother You?

And as I waited through the months
Until You came,
So now I wait for You to come again –
And as I watched You live
And work beside us –
So today You live
And work beside us,
in the body of Your church.

Now in old age I wait –
As in my youth so long ago
I waited
For Your coming –
So as You came to me in time
Out of eternity,
This time You come and take me
To eternity from time.

Come my dearest, come.

A. Seymour

The Millennium Dome

Her belly button sits atop
her pregnant womb
turned inside out
unfurling satin petals
to the gentle sun
while baby feet
make flutters on her skin
and in the royal jelly
of the amniotic sac
her water baby swims
and exercises foetal limbs
preparing to be born.

and now, to show we think
the world of him
we've built a plastic bubble
like a belly button
perched atop a pregnant womb
to celebrate the day
that he was born.

Doesn't it make you wonder
what God sees in us?

Tina Beattie

"How shall I name you then, O You, the Beyond-all-name."

Gregory Nazianzen

O You, Beyond-all-name
  became the Word
    Word of Life
    Word of Truth
    Word of Knowledge

skittering light off darkness
  reflecting
  refracting
  splinters of hope
  opening new vistas
of what maybe in the bleakness of what was
  indeed of what is
  in the Word unheard.

O You, the Beyond-all-name
  not content to remain
  unheard Word
    took our flesh
    became our human form
    embraced our frailty
    accepted our vulnerability
    Could you do more?
      Knowing us
      loving us
      calling us forth   to the more.

Anne Hine, rscj

Luke 8: 43–48

Now there was a woman who had been
suffering from haemorrhages for twelve
years; and though she had spent all she
had on physicians, no one could cure her.
She came up behind him and touched
the fringe of his clothes, and immediately
her haemorrhage stopped. Then Jesus
asked, "Who touched me?" When all
denied it, Peter said, "Master, the crowds
surround you and press in on you." But
Jesus said, "Someone touched me; for I
noticed that power had gone out from me."
When the woman saw that she could not
remain hidden, she came trembling;
and falling down before him, she declared
in the presence of all the people why she
had touched him, and how she had been
immediately healed. He said to her,
"Daughter, your faith has made you well;
go in peace."

A healing touch

Who touched me? Somebody touched me
With the needs, the dreams and the hopes of the world
Who touched me? Somebody touched me
And I turned and saw the people
And I turned and listened to their story
Who touched me? Somebody touched me
And I turned and saw two worlds where God created one
And the gates of the rich were closed

And I dreamed of the world you created
A garden with plenty for everyone
With a stream of clean flowing water
For all to drink

And I believe in life
I believe in hope
I believe in a future where there is one world
Which we build together.

Who touched me? Somebody touched me
And I pray
Stay with us, Lord, as we work for a better world.

Amen.

Linda Jones (CAFOD)

Lord, we pray for those living on the edge of communities:

For women trapped in violent relationships, afraid to leave because they have nowhere safe to take their children, living each day in fear, making the kids keep quiet in case they get hit;
Help us to love one another as you love us

For asylum seekers, often running for their lives and risking everything, yet now facing suspicion, forced to move from place to place, unable to get work or claim benefits;
Help us to love one another as you love us

For young people leaving care, alone and unsupported without the safety net of a family, fending for themselves on the streets;
Help us to love one another as you love us

For those who sleep on the pavement tonight because all the hostels are full;
Help us to love one another as you love us

May we grow in love and faithfulness as we build your new community on earth.

Rachel Lampard and Jennie Richmond (CHAS)

Galatians 5: 13–14

For you were called to freedom, brothers and sisters;
only do not use your freedom as an opportunity for
self-indulgence, but through love become slaves
to one another. For the whole law is summed up in
a single commandment, 'You shall love your
neighbour as yourself'.

Loving God	Duw cariad
we believe	credwn
we are your new creation	mai ni yw dy greadigaethau newydd
born not out of fear and hatred	wedi'n geni, nid o ofn a chasineb
but out of love;	ond o gariad;
we believe	credwn
we are born free,	i ni gael ein geni i ryddid,
free to love and serve	yn rhydd i garu a gwasanaethu
our neighbour	ein cymydog
and each other.	a'n gilydd.
So let us never be ashamed	Felly na fydded gennym gywilydd
of declaring this love	un amser i ddatgan mai'r cariad hwn
as the basis	yw sylfaen
of our lives	ein bywydau
of our church	ein heglwys
and of a fair and just world.	ac i fyd teg a chyfiawn.

Rev. Mair Bowen

Reflection

It is relatively easy to see what is wrong and to reflect on it in faith; it can be much harder to take that reflection into action, and yet this is what we are called as Christians to do, and as Christian women we have a duty to take the fruits of our voluntary actions into the political sphere.

Catherine Shelley for NBCW Study Day, 1996

Chains of Debt

God grant me the spirit of courage, that I may have the strength to
    fight injustice
Give me the spirit of challenge, that I may not accept the status quo
    without question
Give me the spirit of compassion, that I may see the world from
    other people's viewpoint

I ask for the spirit of gentleness, that I may listen to the voice of the
    poor without trampling on their dreams in my rush to action

God grant me your Spirit, the spirit of truth, justice and hope, that I
may rest and work in the vision of a new future, where all are linked
by the bonds of humanity, not enslaved by the chains of debt.

Linda Jones (CAFOD)

Deuteronomy 15: 1–2, 7–8

Every seventh year you shall grant a remission of debts. And this is the manner of remission: every creditor shall remit the claim that is held against a neighbour, not exacting it from a neighbour who is a member of the community, because the Lord's remission has been proclaimed.

If there is among you anyone in need, a member of your community in any of your towns within the land that the Lord your God is giving you, do not be hard-hearted or tight-fisted towards your needy neighbour. You should rather open your hand, willingly lending enough to meet the need, whatever it may be.

There is an enormous variety of gifts and ministries, some of which St Paul spells out in II Corinthians Chapter 12, a chapter to study and be formed by. These same ministries exist to this day but perhaps the difference is we do not always acknowledge them, or appreciate them, as actual calls from God. It is possible that someone who asks uncomfortable and challenging questions of the Church or who is not satisfied with the *status quo*, could be prophetic, not merely a critic.

The saints were by and large unrecognised in their own day. But the early Church worked hard at being parts of the one body, to include and not to exclude.

How about more hidden but essential ministries? Was the early Church not strengthened by the years Mary spent when she *'treasured all these things and pondered them in her heart'?* Today there are indeed many modest and silent souls who remain hidden but who carry on quietly and faithfully praying in the midst of the mysteries and confusion of changes in the Church and the perplexities and sorrows of life.

This is one of the most important ministries of our day, no less vital because it is unrecognised.

It is not by chance that we are living in this exciting time of Jubilee preparation and since God always surprises us, we must be on the alert for new instructions. A new ministry can come to anyone, the teenager still in school, the single mother, the old-age pensioner, someone *'between jobs'* – no extra qualifications are necessary ! God prepares us in His Own unique ways and we are always taken unawares since *"the heavens are as high above the earth as my ways are above your ways, my thoughts above your thoughts."* (Isaiah 55:9)

"If anyone has ears to hear, let him listen to what the Spirit is saying to the Church" (Revelation 2: 7)

Sue Norris

Holy Mother Hilda
we rejoice to follow your example
of obedient reconciliation.
As you in your day sought peace with courage
and strove to preserve the unity of the Church
and the Christian cohesion of our land,
so may we be guided to know when we should resist
and when we should accept
that the Gospel may be proclaimed
and the reconciling love of God revealed.

AMEN.

Edith Reyntiens and Rev. Jean Mayland

John 17: 20

"I ask not only on behalf of these, but also on behalf
of those who will believe in me through their word,
that they may all be one. As you, Father, are in me and
I am in you, may they also be in us, so that the world
may believe that you have sent me."

Millennium Alleluia

Lord of Love,
Wide harbour of patient healing,
Sanctuary of unseen horizons;
In this year unite us forever.

Janet McSwiney

Leviticus 25: 10–12, 15, 30-31, 39-41

And you shall hallow the fiftieth year and you shall proclaim liberty throughout the land to all its inhabitants. It shall be a jubilee for you; you shall return, every one of you, to your property and every one of you to your family. That fiftieth year shall be a jubilee for you; you shall not sow, or reap the aftergrowth,or harvest the unpruned vines. For it is a jubilee; it shall be holy to you: you shall eat only what the field itself produces.

When you buy from your neighbour, you shall pay only for the number of years since the jubilee;the seller shall charge you only for the remaining crop-years.

But if there are not sufficient means to recover it, what has been sold shall remain with the purchaser until the year of jubilee;in the jubilee it will be released, and the property shall be returned.

If it is not redeemed before a full year has elapsed, a house that is in a walled city shall pass in perpetuity to the purchaser, throughout the generations; it shall not be released in the jubilee. But houses in villages that have no walls around them shall be classed as open country; they may be redeemed, and they shall be released in the jubilee.

If any who are dependent on you become so impoverished that they sell themselves to you, you shall not make them serve as slaves. They shall remain with you as hired or bound labourers. They shall serve with you until the year of jubilee. Then they and their children with them shall be free from your authority; they shall go back to their own family and return to their ancestral property.

Compassionate God,
open our hearts
that we may feel the breath and play of your Spirit,
unclench our hands
that we may reach out to one another in openness and generosity,
free our lips
that we may speak for those whose voices are not heard,
unlock our ears
to hear the cries of the broken-hearted,
and open our eyes
to see Christ in friend and stranger,
that in sharing our love and our pain,
our poverty and our prosperity,
we may move towards that peace and justice
which comes from you
and so be bearers of divine reconciliation
Amen

Annabel Shilson-Thomas (CAFOD)

It has been a long journey
this journey we have made together
from beyond the hills of morning
through valleys green and golden
in the sunlight
across the desert reaches
and over ridges steeper
than we cared to climb.
There has been a touch of madness
about it,
surely – or what seems madness –
for we came to the place
strong in this holy company
company of living faith
open the treasure
Give all – pour it out.
This is no time for calculation
no time to ask for guarantee
or safe return on our investment –
let love alone be the measure
for we have further yet to journey.
We must travel lightly who follow the star
in whose hearts are the roads to Zion.

R. Consedine PVBM

Micah 6: 8

and what does the Lord require of you
but to do justice, and to love kindness,
and to walk humbly with your God?

Revelations 21: 1–7

Then I saw a new heaven and a new earth; for the first
heaven and the first earth had passed away, and the sea
was no more. And I saw the holy city, the new Jerusalem,
coming down out of heaven from God, prepared as a
bride adorned for her husband. And I heard a loud
voice from the throne saying,
"See, the home of God is
    among mortals.
He will dwell with them;
they will be his peoples,
and God himself will be with them;
he will wipe every tear from their eyes.
Death will be no more;
mourning and crying and pain will be
    no more,
for the first things have passed away".
And the one who is seated on the throne said,
"See, I am making all things new"

Then he said to me, "It is done ! I am the
Alpha and the Omega, the beginning and
the end. To the thirsty I will give water as
a gift from the spring of the water of life.
Those who conquer will inherit these
things, and I will be their God, and they
will be my children."